Cameos

A Poetry Collection by
Michael Gallowglas

Copyright © 2024 Michael Todd Gallowglas

All rights reserved.

ISBN: 979-8-88627-220-8

BRIAN TURNER

For our ongoing friendship words and taking me seriously when I told him that I wasn't spending over $10K a semester to fuck around.

CONTENTS

The Day Peter Dinklage Drove Me
    to an Attempted Murder—1
Game of Trolls—3
Batters Up—4
A Duel for the Ages—5
Incognito—6
Cowboy Wisdom—7
Escaping the Irish Circle Trap—8
Coffee Questions and a Swift Departure—10
On With the Show—11
A Typecast of Melancholy—12
Voice Over—14
My Turn to Speak—15
Patience—16
A Whole New Jive—17
Dream Bigger—18
What You Don't Know—19
Dead Poet's Road Trip—20
Ontological Blues—21
Misplaced Nostalgia—22
Con-fidence—23
The Show Must Go On the Internet—24
Lessons Learned—30
Aaaaand… Action!—25
What's in a Name?—28
A Re-Imagined Classic—29
Lessons Learned—30
A Jab to the Heart—32
In Medias Res—34
Let's Get Ready to Thumble—35
Stars Struck—37
House Training—38
The Time Peter Dinklage Drove Up
    and Saved Me from Murdering My Darlings—39
The Elephant in the Poem—41

Michael Gallowglas

ACKNOWLEDGMENTS

Patricia Smith taught me I could write about hard truths without confronting them head-on. She also gave me the epiphany that poets are storytellers too. Sometimes a story needs to be a poem more than fiction.

Gailmarie Pahmeier encouraged me to lean into poetry about my nerdy passions and it's okay to revisit certain aspects of our aesthetics in poem after poem after poem.

Lee Herrick kept reminding me that poets are just as free to make things up as fiction writers.

Gayle Brandeis dared me to dive head-first into every surreal adventure my imagination came up with in both fiction and poetry.

Luke, Kat, and Faylita were awesome poetic friends long before I started writing poetry.

Rebecca, my dear friend, is traveling a parallel journey to Frankenstein prose and poetry together because her voice also refuses to be confined to one medium.

The Day Peter Dinklage Drove Me to an Attempted Murder

Sometimes it's best if you don't try
and figure out the weird stuff. As Freud said,
sometimes a cigar is just a cigar. Sometimes,
the weird stuff is pretty self-explanatory.
Take, for example, the dream where my ex
and the first great heartbreak after my ex
sent me an invitation to their wedding.
Of course, I'm going to go and witness
this occasion. However, it was all a ruse
to get me to a secluded mountain cabin.
I would show up. Alone. The ladies
would pull out their Glock 20s, kneecap me,
and execute me *Heat* style. Not a big stretch
to figure out what my subconscious
was doing from that dram. I suffered
that dream for months, repeating, over
and over on repeat and over again.
I'd always wake up hyperventilating.
But then... one time... I was in the limo,
heading up to the cabin... Helping myself
to the bar when I noticed Peter Dinklage
up front in the driver's seat. That was new.
I asked: *What are you doing in my dream?*
His classically-trained actor's eyes glanced
into the rear-view mirror, and he replied:
I'm Peter Dinklage, I do whatever the fuck I want.
Hard to argue with that, so I enjoyed
the limo drive up to yet another execution.
We arrived at the secluded cabin. I walked
down the path as slowly as the dream allowed.
As always, my ex and the first great heartbreak

after my ex waited with their Glock 20s.
Let's get this over with so I can wake up
hyperventilating... again... except...
When the ladies whipped out their Glock 20s,
Peter Dinklage jumped out of my pants,
grabbed their Glocks, and pistol-whipped
them like Ray Liotta in Goodfellas.
I stared and stammered, *What the Fuck?*
Peter Dinklage fixed me with his classically-trained
actor's eyes and said: *I told you.*
I'm Peter Dinklage I do what the fuck I want.
Sometimes it's best if you don't try
and figure out the weird stuff. Sometimes
Peter Dinklage jumping out of your pants
is just Peter Dinklage jumping out of your pants.

Game of Trolls

I finagled my way
into the Rave of Thrones
after-party at Comic-Con
by convincing the door guy
that I knew George RR Martin.
(I do, but this poem isn't about him.)
They gave me a VIP badge.
The VIP section had an open bar.
Completely opened for the first
90 minutes. Even the top shelf.
I waited and paced myself, until:
Last call for open bar! I ordered
a double shot of 30-year-old MacCallen
(because VIP section open bars will cut you
off if you order too much of the good stuff.)
I turned around and came face to face
with Kit Harrington and Maisie Williams,
and my semi-drunk brain commanded:
Don't pass this up. The stars looked
at me looking at them. They waited
for me to fanboy. I looked
at Maisie Williams, dropped
into my Irish accent, and stage whispered:
I hear your brother doesn't know shit.
Maisie Williams fell over laughing.
I walked away. Kit Harrington
blinked with the expression
of someone wondering how the hell
he got trolled in the VIP section
of the Rave of Thrones party.

Michael Gallowglas

Batters Up

Someday, years from now, I'll be sitting
at the Brooklyn Center for Fiction,
working on some story or other,
and a sound will grow in the background—
soft at first, then it will rise and rise
until it will hit just the right frequency
as the fillings in my teeth. The fillings will buzz
into my mind, creating a whole new kind
of sound that will nearly drown the screams,
screams that will draw everyone outside.
Screams that will draw everyone down
to the East River. Dread Cthulu himself
will rise from the waters, intent
on destroying New York City as his conquest.
His first target will be Lady Liberty.
He'll break our spirits by breaking that monument.
A bright flash will appear in the sky,
only, it won't go away, that flash, bright
as the sun, and Gregorian, rag-time hymns
will drown the alien frequency buzzing
through our fillings and into our minds.
A spiritual subway car will fly out
of that perpetual flash, carrying
Jacky Robinson and Babe Ruth from Heaven.
Those two legendary swingers will leap
out of that spiritual subway car and swing away
with their holy baseball bats of righteousness.
Chthulu won't stand a chance. Those sluggers
will slug dread Cthulu back to the depths
chunk by battered chunk, and I'll head back
to the Brooklyn Center for Fiction
and finish working on some story or other.

A Duel for the Ages

Watching the moon rise on the solstice
in a summer of nostalgia that never existed,
Dr. Andy and I savored velveteen-smooth
whiskey out of crystalline thistle glasses
on the patio at De'Veres Irish Pub,
despite De'Vere's closing down and never
having opened a pub on the outskirts
of Cork. After our fourth or fifth shots,
our heads swam full of widdershins warmth.
Flann O'Brien and W.B. Yeats strolled
out of the mists. Each writer carried
a rapier under his arm as an academic
might nonchalantly carry an umbrella.
Those Irish gentlemen came to our table.
Will you be my second? Flann O'Brien
asked me. W.B. Yates offered Dr. Andy
the same request. Unable to refuse
such august personages or bring ourselves
to miss such an event, we agreed.
The next dawn, we storytellers and poets,
gathered upon Brian Boru's caern.
Flann O'Brien and W.B. Yates faced off
with quill-sharpened swords and carved
grand new masterpieces into each other's flesh.
They departed before Dr. Andy or I
manage to transcribe a single bloody word.
Dr. Andy and I returned to De'Vere's,
raised our crystalline thistle glasses,
and enjoyed our fifth or sixth shots
of velveteen, nostalgia-smooth whiskey.

Incognito

Ryan Reynolds roams during Comic Con
With the cheapest Deadpool costume on.
All through the day
he photo-bombs cosplay
and fades into the crowd — Poof, gone!

Cowboy Wisdom

On my darkest day in the 2020 COVID winter,
someone knocked completely un-Poe-like
on my front door. No tapping, rapping,
or scratching. A simple repetition of three
knocks. Assertive. Full of authority.
Strange, as the doorbell wasn't broken.
John Wayne and Sam Elliott regarded me
up and down. The Duke said:
Take a walkabout with us.
Those two cowboys and I strode along
the green belt next to my home.
Every time I tried to ask a question
one or both of them would hush me,
and we'd keep walking, almost strutting,
somber as gunslingers at high noon.
I imagined spurs going *ching, ching, ching*
on concrete paths winding through the grass.
We stopped at a BBQ pit. Sam Elliott lit a fire.
The Duke lit a cigar. The smoke intermingled.
We drank sarsaparilla from battered tin cups.
Silence hung around us the whole time
like a noose dangling in an empty coffin.
Many grave hours later, I headed for home
all by my lonesome. When I returned,
I built a fire and dismantled my doorbell.

Escaping the Irish Circle Trap

Sunday mornings with coffee are times
for reflection. This morning, Memory takes
me back, back, and back again
to the Black Point Renaissance Faire
when I spied I met Weird
Al. Mr. Yankovic came toward me
with a smoking hot, like Maxim cover model hot,
lady on his arm.
This was the first time my mind ever said:
Don't pass this up.
I stopped Weird Al and used the heel
of my boot to draw a circle
in the dirt and gravel around him.
       I explained: *You are now in an Irish circle trap.*
       You cannot leave until you determine
       the secret of the Irish circle trap.
Weird Al regarded me with bewilderment.
       I am in a trap? he asked.
       I nodded. *Indeed.*
       And I can't get out until I figure out the secret
       of getting out?
       I nodded again. *That is indeed your dilemma.*
Weird Al continued to gaze at me,
though his expression shifted to dumbfounded
admiration.
His mouth opened.
       His mouth closed.
             His mouth opened.
In one of the proudest moments of my life,
Weird Al Yankovic pointed at me, and said:
       You're really weird.
Ultimately, the smoking hot,

and apparently wicked smart lady.
figured out the secret of the Irish circle trap.
She grabbed Weird Al's arm and dragged him away,
ignoring the Irish madman who had trapped
that icon of his childhood in the first place.

Coffee Questions and a Swift Departure

I'm on a coffee date with Taylor Swift.
Randomly, I ask, *Who would you want
to narrate your life?* Taytay sips
her coffee and contemplates.
Morgan Freeman with Sam Jackson's vocabulary.
Tay Tay asks: *Who is your favorite female
vocalist? And you can't pick me.*
It's my turn to sip my coffee, mostly
for the effect rather than needing to stall.
Diana Krall. Does Taylor's expression change
because she's impressed or does my
response come across as a cop-out?
Does Taylor know who Diana Krall is?
My turn. I look deep into Taylor's eyes.
Who is your favorite writer? And you can't pick me.
I am. I write and sing exactly the kind of songs I love.
I almost give Taylor a that's-a-cop-out look,
but then I remember I write exactly
the kind of books and poems I like to read.
One of Taylor's bodyguards whispers in her ear.
I have to go, she says. *I'll text you later.*
I wait and wait and wait, but I never
get a text. Months later, my daughter
adds, "I'll Text You Later,"
by Taylor Swift to our Spotify playlist.

On With the Show

Opening night, and Lin-Manuel Miranda
welcomes me backstage for the coin toss.
Each night, for the musical *Gallowglas*,
the arch nemesis of my life will change.
Patton Oswalt stands ready to play George RR Martin.
John Travolta is eager to test his range
in the role of Brandon Sanderson.
Nathan Fillion shakes my hand and raves about
how much my books have changed his life.
He's going to be me, with Neil Patrick Harris
whisper-singing in his ear the whole show
as Poindexter, the dark voice of my BPD.
Felicia Day is cast as my ex-wife,
completing this horrible reunion.
It's opening night. I am a little punch drunk,
but not on whiskey, for once. I'm Gallowglas,
about to watch *Gallowglas the Musical*.
Lin Manuel tosses a coin. The coin flips.
Everyone holds their breath.
Lin Manuel misses the coin.
The coin rolls into a crack.
Everyone holds their breath.
That's the only coin anyone brought.
My storyteller's brain clicks on.
I cry: *Dueling villains!*
Patton Oswald and John Travolta nod.
Lin Manuel claps. *Yes! Dueling villains!*
Let's make it work! We're professionals!
I take my box seats to enjoy my show.

A Typecast of Melancholy

I wander from cliche to cliche.
Really, they're bars,
but I identify as an Irish writer,
so cliches it is.
Besides, I'm leaning into the classic,
write what you know.
So, cliched bars it is.
Besides, what else am I going to do
once Alex Trebek tells everyone
at trivia night to, *Suck it*, and takes
his questions with him back to heaven?
Bar to bar.
Drink to drink.
Cliche to cliche.
With the agenda to morally bankrupt
my credit card, kidneys, and liver.
A musical note floats
in the Wednesday night fog,
grabs my earlobe, and drags me
to an open bar on the waterfront.
Hugh Laurie sits at the piano,
fingers softly caressing St. James Infirmary
out of the keys. The bartender
has a Beyond the Pale waiting for me.
It's the only drink on the bar.
Another cliche it is.
One more won't hurt,
and I can't tell if I mean
the cliche or the drink.
I swallow both booze and cliche
and gaze over the rim of my empty glass
at the emptier dance floor

and wonder if a certain lady
ever wonders about all the dances
we never got the chance to dance.
I set my former Beyond the Pale down,
tip well, snap three times to Hugh Laurie,
and wander off to My Next Cliche,
because I hear the bartenders there
pour every drink extra heavy.
And so, cliches it is.

Voice Over

Andy Serkis reads
my no context for you tweets
as Gollum. Precious!

My Turn to Speak

I drink Irish coffee and revel
on the divine experience
of Dorothy Parker and Bukowski
trading barbs back and forth.
Dorothy's tongue: sharp, sly, and stinging.
Bukowski's words: blunt, bludgeoning, bullying.
Of course, Dorothy Parker being
Dorothy Parker gives better than she gets.
I drink Irish coffee and score keep.
In mid-assault, Dorothy stops, mid-word.
Pardon me a moment, Charles dear.
The hero of my hero regards me.
This is all well and good, Michael dear.
But even among all this silliness
don't you have something to say?

Patience

How long are you going to stare at that page?
Harlan asks from just over my right shoulder,
but that doesn't mean he won't get sinister.
I reply: *As long as it takes.*
We've had this argument before, Harlan and I,
about when a writer is writing,
and when a writer is just pretending
to be a writer. Like fighting with Joshua
from *War Games,* I've learned
the best strategy is not to play Harlan's games,
or I can change the rules.
You want to change my productivity levels?
In the words of a cantankerous old writer,
fuck you pay me!
Completely out of character, Harlan hushes.
I have sympathy for this devilish caricature
of a man lurking behind me. After all,
I still have tangible fingertips
which makes writing a little easier
for me than this spectre of my mind
created from his books, interviews,
and convention legends. I don't understand
how he sauntered out of my subconscious
to be my Jiminy Cricket with a sledgehammer.
How long are you going to stare at that page?
I give him the same answer I always give:
As long as it takes.
Harlan snorts. *Amateur.*
I shrug. *At least I can write.*
I'm glad he can't throttle me.
I go back to staring at the page
for as long as it takes.

A Whole New Jive

It's one o'clock and I jump
into a jitterbug stroll
all the way to the time
Stephen told me:
*Keep your distance
from the community.*
Nobody seems to care about
these Shim Shim blues shuffling
all the way to this fever burning
from wishing on a star for one last chat
with Frankie Manning and Norma Miller
could set my jive back to groovin.
Frankie might remind me:
    *It ain't what you do,
    it's the way that you do it.*
Norma will add:
    *Yes and sometimes that's the problem.
    You dig?*
I dig. I definitely dig.
Sometimes the way that you do it
is the core of the problem. Stephen
definitely became the problem.
More like, he finally got caught.
How much of what I did
was part of the problem?
How long does it take
for a man to forgive himself
for the missteps of his youth?
In the now, all I can do
is try real hard to dance
new rhythms into my world.

Dream Bigger

I sway gently on the swings down
the greenbelt from my house in suburbia.
I'm trying to return to simpler times
when I wore the blissful blinders of childhood.
Dr King swings next to me. We don't talk.
What would I say? What words could
my imagination possibly do that orator justice?
We sway in alternating rhythms—
forward; up; down; backward—
have I dreamed big enough?
Have I dared to live in such a way
to earn this man's absolution.
Dr. King says nothing.
The breeze picks up. I swing
higher and higher into a dream
where I don't imagine this man looking
over my shoulder, never judging.
Each man's journey is his own.
With Dr. King's lack of judgment,
I'll feel like I never lived
up to his dream. So, I'll swing higher
and higher, to achieve escape velocity
from a harsh, self-imposed reality
Dr King never asked me to adopt.
Forward; up; down; backward—
I'll swing into a dream,
where I can wear child-like blinders.
But I know, eventually, Dr King will call
me back down to earth where his dream
waits for the content of my character.

What You Don't Know

Shielded behind a Mack-the-Knife
grin Count Basie offers me:
Pick a note—any note.
JD Salinger scowls in his solitude:
Pick a word—any word.
At first, I can't comprehend
why these two cats are colliding
in the context of my moment.
But I catch the hint of a recollection—
Holden Caulfield was a dancer.
Like me, he boogied his way out
of his trauma. Or, at least, like
 me... he tried. His jukin
and jivin only provided
a momentary salve, just like for me.
Did you know Holden Caulfield was a dancer?
I didn't catch that. Not the first time,
not until my second time through the story,
and that was only after Basie's genius
had infected my feet. What else
am I not catching in classic stories
because of things that aren't on my radar?

Dead Poet's Road Trip

Driving through an autumn
wood of leafless trees.
Anne Sexton rides shotgun.
Hemingway grumbles in inarticulate,
butt-hurt syllables in the back seat
and refuses to buckle his seat belt.
He wants to stop for a drink,
despite a complete and total lack
of any towns much less bars.
The road winds next to a stream
desperately trying to become a river.
Perhaps after the snow melts.
I glance into the rear-view.
Virginia Woolf trudges out of shallow
cold waters. I pull over, shift into reverse,
and ask: *Need a lift?* She regards
the only open sea next to Hemingway.
Virginia says: *I'll take the next one.*
Before I open my mouth, she sneers.
I'm sure. I'm earnest when I kick
Hemingway to the curb. Later,
we agree, Anne, Virginia, and me,
to invite Sylvia Plath to take the final
seat when we come across her
at a solitary BBQ. I drive, and drive,
through this autumn wood of leafless trees
slightly less symbolic than these poets.
I wonder, can my metaphor and poem
ever reach its satisfying conclusion?

Ontological Blues

Emmanuel Kant and I went to visit Plato
which is a lot like mashing up sets between
Lord of the Rings and *Clash of the Titans*,
expansive and underground, but homey with columns.
Plato accuses: *Your hubris is near limitless.*
His assertion stems from my ontological belief
that my cameo poems create new existences
where I am the star. Kant shakes his head.
Existence cannot be measured by transitory entities.
I reply: *I exhibit various qualities without
exhausting the totality of my hubris.*
Descartes wanders by. Kant invites
him to join us. Descartes replies,
I think not, and disappears.
I reach for paper and pens
in a mad rush to justify
my existence
to my Self.

Misplaced Nostalgia

Someone hit the reset button
on my neighborhood last night.
Today's morning walk takes me
through vacant lots and fields of weeds
rather than endless suburban purgatory.
Back at the house, Dad's shouting for me.
Again. Something crashes and breaks. Again.
I walk all day, sneak water from faucets
in random yards when no one's around
the way I did during summer vacations.
the sun lazily drifts downward.
I meander for a while past dark.
Foxtails get caught in my socks.
My journey takes me down to the levee,
and I cross paths with River Phoenix
as young Indiana Jones. He smiles.
I'm going to find a body. Wanna come?
I wish him well, but I have enough
problems with this body. Sometime around
midnight, the street lights flicker on.
Time to go home. Maybe tomorrow things
will revert back to normal rather than
devolving into yesterday's status quo.

Con-fidence

Surprise interactions are the best parts of conventions.
Like the time David Gerald invited me to dinner
at the World Science Fiction Convention. On a whim,

I said: *Tell me something about Harlan Ellison,*
because I know David and Harlan were close,
and David knows I admire Harlan's work.

David told Harlan stories all evening. He also talked
about Robin Williams, William Shatner, and an epic
Saturday Night Live sketch no one will ever see.

In the elevator heading to parties, I wondered,
Do I know things I'm not supposed to know?
If you have questions about what I know,

you won't be the first, and I'll tell you what
I tell everyone else who asks. Sometimes, the sign
of real friendship is knowing when you don't

have to ask to keep something in confidence.
    However,
I'll happily describe the shenanigans that happened
in exacting detail when John Scalzi happened by.

The Show Must Go On the Internet

I'm encased in a minuscule black-box theater:
four black walls, a black ceiling, black floor.
The only anomalies: three rows of empty
brown-leather chairs and my white and gray
sports coat. I sit on a black chair, center stage.
The show is over, but I replay it inside my head.
Robert Preston enters with no fanfare from stage left,
a parade of one without a single trumpet
let alone any number of trombones.
He asks: *How'd it go kid?* I reply: *Not too shabby
for what it was intended to be.* Preston nods.
Will you ever do it again? I contemplate.
Every time I post something personal on social media.
After all, the whole internet's a stage.
That's gonna be a hell of a run, kid,
Preston says: *Don't forget to go dark
every now and then.* My turn to nod.
Every time my voice needs a break.
And by that, I'm not talking about talking.
Break a leg, kid, Preston says. *Break a leg.*

Aaaaand... Action!

You're filming a documentary about Gallowglas,
and you follow him to Comic Con,
and that first morning he sits outside
the Starbucks where he likes to people-watch
and pimp his books. He says: *I'm gonna
chill here. You can go get other footage.*
But you decide to keep the camera rolling...
...
CM Punk wanders by, grabs the seat next to
Gallowglas, and they talk details about turning
Gallowglas's *Team Red Hand* stories into a Netflix
series.
Gallowglas says: *I have to write it first.*
CM punk puts Gallowglas in the Anaconda Vice then
hits him with the GTS.
So Gallowglas is lying there unconscious...
...
And you keep the camera rolling...
...
Neve Campbell rushes out of the gawking crowd and
screams at Gallowglas until he wakes up. She buys
him enough coffee for a party of five, and they talk
about her playing the role of Jenny Everywhere in the
film version of *Hush*.
Gallowglas says: *I have to write it first.*
Neve Campbell screams at Gallowglas to finish and
leaves. He drinks the coffee she got him.
...
And you keep the camera rolling...
...
Gallowglas Jims the camera:
I kinda already promised

*that part to Anna Kendrick,
but I have to write it first.*

...

And you keep the camera rolling...

...

Ronald Moore slows down long enough to remind Gallowglas that *Outlander* is wrapping up and they need to talk about the magical surrealism sword and planet spin-off from *Spellpunk*.
Gallowglas calls after him: I *have to write it first.*

...

And you keep the camera rolling...

...

Chris Pratt struts up with a classic boom box and challenges Gallowglas to a dance-off. Bro! Luckily, Heather Graham is grabbing some coffee, and so Gallowglas and Graham swing out across the sidewalk and slaughter Chris Pratt's solo moves. Chris Pratt asks when they're gonna do that remake of *Strictly Ballroom*.
Gallowglass replies: *I have to write it first.*

...

And you keep the camera rolling...

...

Gallowglas drinks more coffee...

...

Nathan Fillion stops. He sits, and he and Gallowglas talk for hours and hours about all the nerdy things they're into without even hinting at the things that would make this golden.
For the first time, you prompt: what about *Firefly* or *Doctor Horrible*?
Fillion and Gallowglas stare at you...

...

And you keep the camera rolling...

Cameos

...
And they stare at you...
...
And you keep the camera rolling...
...
And Neil Patrick Harris strolls up and reminds
Nathan Fillion they have that press thing. Nathan asks
Gallowglas: *We're still good for that* Freaky Friday,
Groundhog Day, *and* Twins *mash-up, right?*
Gallowglas shrugs: *It depends on when Schwarzenegger finishes writing it.*
...
You call: *Cut*!
and turn the camera off.

What's in a Name?

My mother's dog barks in the backyard
and reminds me of all the dogs I've called
friend. Contemplating companions past
and who they're named after,
Scrappy, my first, Scooby Doo's cousin;
Frankie, after Frankie Manning;
Dante, for the poet;
Faelin, after one of my characters;
Jack, the last, with that big black spot
lolling on his tongue. Whenever he
bounds out of my memories, my fingers
itch to scratch his night-dark fur.
I wonder if my minuscule modicum
of celebrity will warrant anyone
ever honoring me in such a way.
Queue Geoffry Rush as Barbosa
from *Pirates of the Caribbean:*
We named the monkey Gallowglas.

    shrug   I'll take it.

A Re-Imagined Classic

Two electric candles glow on a grand piano.
The rest of the bar is dark. The second
piano pouts in silence without candles
to let the nonexistent audience know
it's there too. In the darkest corner
at the end of the marble-white bar,
Diana Krall's fingers tap out a new
arrangement for "Baby Shark," as if written
by Duke Ellington and sung by Billie Holiday.
If the pianos could react, how might they
respond to being the first instrument
to bring that reimagined song into a world
that never asked for such a... a... thing.
I sip my extra-chocolaty organic stout.
I ask Diana Krall: *Why?* Her fingers
never stop moving. She responds:
Have you never tried to write something
just to see if you can? I take a long draw
off my extra-chocolaty organic stout.
Do my journals ever react
to my narrative experiments
the way these pianos can't
under the threat of producing
Diana Krall's potential song?

Lessons Learned

Kicking up leaves during my morning walk
to stir up a subject worthy of a poem.

Every synapse fires back to the new lady
who has completely inhabited my imagination.

I want every word to punctuate
innuendos into her everything.

Carrie Fisher shows up in clothing
appropriate to the early spring weather.

Hiking boots, jeans, hoodie, jacket.
Carrie punches my arm. *Knock that shit off.*

This time, Cool Space Aunt doesn't
let me get a word in edgewise.

Her middle finger raises between us,
silencing me as completely as a force choke.

Once, shame on her. Twice, shame on you.
How many times have you gone through this?

I don't answer because I don't want
her to smack the back of my head.

Frank Oz's voice flows out of Carrie's mouth.
      Patience.

And now I'm kicking up leaves and walking home
alone to write this far more productive poem

rather than an overly cliche cheese fest
about a not-romance I won't remember
by the time I get around to editing this.

Michael Gallowglas

A Jab to the Heart

The Goodwill next
to my daughter's gymnastics
classes has a vending
machine that offers
wild cherry Pepsi.
It's a treat I allow
myself as a reward
for being a good father.
Today, I wait behind
a line of one,
an older gentleman
takes his time
contemplating his choice
of carbonated beverage.
I'm not in a rush,
so I don't bother him.
He finally chooses Mt. Dew
and turns around.
Doctor Fauci.
I haven't thought about him
in… in… how long?
Maybe not since
my last shot.
He looks at me,
looking at him.
He recognizes that I
recognize him. He waits
for me to decide
how I'm going
to react. That man
has been revered
and reviled by so many.

I smile, say, *Thanks man*,
and move around
him to get my
wild cherry Pepsi
I hope his life
has returned to some
semblance of peace.

In Medias Res

Stan Lee and Jack Kirby
ride my shoulders, switching
back and forth between
being angel the demon.

Except, they never reveal
which of them is giving
which kind of advice.

Reverse psychology permeates
their puppet-mastery machinations
to make me the perfect
representation of hero and villain—
depending on momentary perspectives.

I keep asking: *What's my superpower?*
They reply: *You're like us.*
They go back to murmuring.

Pushing buttons.
Pulling strings.

Dancing me to one random event
to another to the next in my
never-ending origin story.

Let's Get Ready to Thumble

The crowd cleared a wide circle
in the middle of the Comic Con
exhibitor hall. Two seemingly ageless
men stalked each other in that wide
barren space. A hush fell.
Daniel Radcliffe and Elijah Wood.
Elijah Wood and Daniel Radcliffe.
Circled, circled, rounded, squared,
and metaphorically octagoned off.
Their hands came up and fingers
locked together. *Gentlemen,*
I said wearing my black and white
referee shirt. Are you ready
to thumb war? Glaring eyes
and clenched teeth gave me
the only response I needed.
Mortal Kombat-like, I declared,
FIGHT! Still, they glared.
Daniel Radcliffe and Elijah Wood.
Elijah Wood and Daniel Radcliffe.
Thumbs poised upright and unmoving.
The crowd remained as still
as those unwarring thumbs.
The gravitational constant
of the universe froze, cascading
out from those thumb warriors
who had yet to begin their conflict.
Elsewhere in the multiverse
civilizations crumbled, species
went extinct, and versions of me
wept for not knowing the glory
of those ageless men glaring,

wild-grinning, thumbs unwarring.
Daniel Radcliffe and Elijah Wood.
Elijah Wood and Daniel Radcliffe.
Finally, those ageless men nodded,
and said: *I found out what I needed
to know.* They released each other's hand,
bowed, and faded into the Comic Con
crowd. Next! I said. Two massive nerds
stepped into that metaphorical Octagon.
And I mean MASSIVE nerds.
Terry Crews. Vin Diesel. Locked hands.
Vin Diesel. Terry Crews. Thumbs poised.
No universe is prepared for this
much nerdy awesomeness.

Stars Struck

What's going on outside my window?
A squirrel happily munches away
on some nut or other morsel;
John Cena bursts out of the hedge
and power slams the little guy into
the rose bushes; Axel Rose paradises
John Cena's attitude with a bit
of jungle juice; Carl Douglas wages
a not-so-civil war against Axle Rose
and buries him in the backyard;
Keanu Reeves kung fus Carl Douglas
through the oak tree next door;
Alan Rickman yippee ki yays
Keanu Reeves into the green waste
bin at the edge of the sidewalk;
Will Smith wraps Alan Rickman
in red silk and declares him
an independent state;
James Earl Jones force chokes
his way into the fray and lulls
everyone into being chill
with that deep, hypnotic voice;;;
Of course, none of that's real.
But that's what happens on mornings
when my imagination gets squirrelly.

House Training

My dog keeps peeing
in one corner of the family room.
She used to pee in the hall
until I ripped the carpet out.
Two trainers invite themselves
into my house. Steve Irwin and Joe Exotic
offer their best solutions.
Gentle affections in setting firm boundaries.
Shock collar that bitch. She'll learn.
The argument gets loud, heated, physical.
I find out Steve Irwin is not as gentle
with people as he is with animals.
I bet you're wondering which bits
of this poem are real and which bits
are metaphors. I'll let you wonder.
Just like I let Steve and Joe fight.
My dog just peed in the corner.
Again. And I gotta clean it up.

The Time Peter Dinklage Drove Up and Saved Me from Murdering My Darlings

The last time Peter Dinklage showed up
in one of my poems, things got weird.
Today's poem is going to get meta
with a side helping of surreal. I'm flipping
through this last month of cameo poems,
reflecting upon the ratio of silly to profound
and contemplating each poem's worthiness
in the vast canon of American letters.
Peter Dinklage drives up in the limo
from the last poem he decided to visit.
I don't ask. Peter Dinklage does whatever
the fuck he wants. Peter joins me and says:
*That's a severe expression you've got while reading
those poems. Are they any good?* I shrug.
*One already got published. The others...
I don't know.* I go on about juggling
the joy of writing and wanting people
to take me seriously as a poet. I ask:
Did you ever feel that way as an actor?
Peter Dinklage rubs his chin, contemplative.
*I only took roles I would enjoy or further my career.
I never let myself be typecast as the little man actor.*
I nod and think of his body of work:
Game of Thrones, X-Men, Knights of Badassdom.
(That's a real movie btw.) Superbowl commercials.
and his total badassery in *Cyrano de Bergerac,*
Peter Dinklage goes inside and returns
with a cup of Death Wish coffee. I raise
my Boba Fett coffee mug, and tell him:
I never dreamed that dream again after that night.
Peter Dinklage, Nightmare Slayer. We savor

Death Wish coffee. (A real brand I just adore.)
and discuss past projects that made our creative
hearts sing. Eventually, Peter Dinklage says:
I'm needed back on set. You figure things out?
I thumb the poems I wrote this month,
contemplate, and nod. *Yeah. I got this.*
Peter Dinklage gets in the limo and leaves
me alone with my coffee and poems.
I lift the journal full of blank pages,
pages waiting for my multi-colored pens,
to my nose and draw in a deep breath
of unrealized poetic potential. I declare
in a stage whisper: *I'm Michael Todd Gallowglas.*
I write about whatever the fuck I want.

The Elephant in the Poem

My writing journey never ends. Like Alexander Hamilton, I'm never satisfied. I'll never be satisfied. I'm totally okay with that. It keeps me going. It keeps me from getting bored. It keeps me pushing my writing into places I never expected. Those unexpected detours into new paths and side quests I never saw coming are some of the greatest joys of my professional and creative life.

This book is the first of a dozen poetry collections I plan to write in 2024. Every leap year gets a flash fiction a day and a poem a day. For 2024, each month of poems gets a new theme. In the summer of 2023, I started playing around with a poem about Peter Dinklage interrupting a recurring dream. Until January 1st, 2024, I'd never written that poem down. I just riffed every time I performed it at open mic nights. When the time came to start a year's worth of poems, I decided to call January's theme, *Cameos*. All the poems I wrote in January 2024 would have appearances by famous people: pop culture icons, literary figures, or personages of historical significance. The first couple of poems were silly and whimsical. Of course, I started with Peter Dinklage, as he inspired the collection. I felt the whole month would go like that, just silly and whimsical poetry about famous people and surreal situations. Some of them may be based on reality, as I've met a handful of famous people in whimsical and surreal situations.

The poems kept getting more and more surreal. I was having a blast. I could totally keep this up for a month.

And then...

My subconscious spoke to me through Dorothy Parker. In a poem, she asked me what I had to say.

I thought about that.

What did I have to say? What could I talk about through these famous people? Maybe I could talk about some heavy subjects without addressing those heavy subjects head-on. I even flipped through the poems I'd already written in the journal and saw the early stages of that idea in them. I'd planted seeds. Now I needed to water and cultivate this new garden.

Throughout January of 2024, I wrote about: depression, toxic masculinity, problematic role models, not living up to one's potential, friendships, the cult of personality, and many many others. With each poem, I tried my best to keep the deeper subjects hidden under layers of celebrities and language. I didn't want anyone to be able to point at any of the poems after a first read and be able to say, this is what the poem is about. If I did my job right, people who read the poems without reading this essay will ever be able to point at any of the poems and say, "It's about this..." Well, they might, and they'll probably be both a little right and a little wrong.

In the thirty-one poems in this book, I've explored the skill of writing about something through writing about something completely other than the something I'm writing about. I've done that unintentionally in fiction before, noticing it in hindsight when readers pointed it out to me. Here, through the rough drafts and edits, I've worked to do it intentionally. Some of the poems succeeded more than others. I'm excited to play around with this new gadget and my toolbox. As of this writing, I still have over 200 poems this year for experimentation.

For me, the best poetry is—heck, the best writing—offers accessibility on the surface with a completely satisfying experience of the first read, but it leaves enough clues, hints, and nudges to invite the reader into a deeper exploration to find out what else is in there. Sometimes a poem doesn't have to be about more than Jackie Robinson and Babe Ruth saving New York with their holy baseball bats of righteousness or Ryan Reynolds goofing off at Comic Con. The world needs those poems as well as the poems that trick us into thinking more deeply about the world. If we can do both, then we've got something special going on in our imaginations. that might, just might, get something special going on in the imaginations of those who experience our work.

Thanks for experiencing my cameo poems.

MICHAEL TODD GALLOWGLAS

Start with raw imagination. Add two parts coffee to every one-part whiskey (for best results, use irish or Scottish single malts. Bourbon may result in a volatile mess.)

Add equal heaping spoonfuls of angst, whimsy, snark, and just a dash of imposter syndrome. Shake vigorously. Once it stops frothing, drop in one master of fine arts in fiction and a second in poetry. Sprinkle a healthy dose of shenanigans on top, while chanting either, "What's a gleeman?" Or, "tell me a story," depending on personal taste.

Yields one pantheon, a faerie war, a cloak of tales, the thwarting of devils and demons, revolutions, slightly above-average misadventures, nerdy poetry, convention panels, geek literary theory, writing classes, role-playing games, airsoft battles (because it's cooler than paintball), and groovy swing dancing. Best served at con temperature.

A man known by his friends to be a bit too clever for his own good, Michael Todd Gallowglas is a hybrid-author (with mainstream and alternative publications), storyteller, and educator from Northern California. He has written over 20 books including novels, short story collections, poetry collections, and non-fiction books. He holds a Bachelor of Arts in Creative Writing from San Francisco State University, a Master of Fine Arts in Fiction from Sierra Nevada College, and a Master in Fine Arts in Poetry from the University of Nevada Reno,

Tahoe. His traditional storytelling show at Renaissance Faires, Celtic Festivals, and geeky conventions has mesmerized audiences for over thirty years. When not writing, Gallowglas is an avid gamer, enjoys ballroom dancing (swing, blues, and tango are his favorites), and adores coffee. Lots and lots of coffee.

Michael Gallowglas

Cameos

Made in the USA
Columbia, SC
23 February 2025